£3.00

Printed and Published in Great Britain by D. C. THOMSON & CO., LTD.,
185 Fleet Street, London, EC4A 2HS.
© D. C. THOMSON & CO., LTD., 1989
ISBN 0-85116-454-4

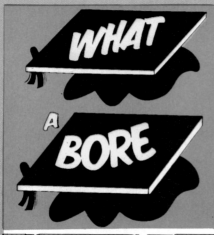

UNWANTED GIFTS

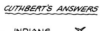

HAW! THAT'S THE DAFTEST THING YOU'VE EVER DONE, SMIFFY!

NIFF

OH, NO, T ISN'T...

OO-ER!

...REMEMBER THE TIME WE BROKE TEACHER'S CAR WINDSCREEN...

...SMIFFY BOARDED IT UP! HAR-HAR-HAR!

SHRIEK!

JUST AS WELL HE HAS SUCH A THICK HEAD!

THAT'S NOT THE DAFTEST THING HE'S EVER DONE...

I'LL TAKE YOUR PICTURE, PLUG!

...REMEMBER WHEN HE GOT A NEW INSTANT CAMERA...

...HE WAS TOLD TO TAKE SOME PILLS IN WATER, SO HE DID!

GURGLE! BURBLE!

NOT AS DAFT AS WHEN HE WAS TOLD TO DRY THE DISHES...

WE DISAGREED OVER THE DAFTEST THING SMIFFY'S EVER DONE!

HAW-HAW! THAT'S THE DAFTEST THING I'VE EVER HEARD OF PEOPLE FIGHTING ABOUT!

HAR-HAR!

It's my dearest wish to win the inter-school tug-of-war contest, just for once!

Soon—

Right, boys—pull!

Well, you've got to start in a small way and work up!

I know—we'll tr... on school custa...

On the way to the contest—

We've never been fitter! We're sure to win!

My chompers feel fine now!

Slurp! In fact, they need exercise!

Erk! Stop him—we'll never get him out of that place!

So—

Gosh! They must be strong... hungry Fatty's harder to s... than a charging rhino!

Bah!

So—

PULL!

Grunt! Snort! Gnn!

Scream! That face! We can't stand it!

Blob Street win!

...ST TRAIN HARD FOR THIS ...S TUG-OF-WAR CONTEST!

I GET PLENTY PRACTICE TUGGING MY HAIR!

TUG TUG

FIRST WE NEED A GOOD ANCHOR MAN...

I KNOW THE VERY FELLOW!

DIM

MY UNCLE BARNABAS WOULD MAKE A GREAT ANCHOR MAN!

PIECES OF SEVEN! PIECES OF SEVEN!

EVEN SMIFFY'S UNCLE'S PARROT ALWAYS GETS THINGS WRONG!

SWOON

ONE, TWO—HEAVE!

CHEEK!

SOMEWHAT THICK SCHOOL CUSTARD

On the day of the contest—

I'LL HAVE TO WITHDRAW FROM THE TEAM—I'VE GOT DREADFUL TOOTHACHE!

So—

GULP!

OUCH!

OUCH!

PING!

THERE YOU GO, FATTY!

...essing-room—

...T, BOYS—GO OUT THERE ...AND WIN, FOR THE ...NOUR OF BASH STREET!

ERK! WE'VE LOST ALL OUR STRENGTH—CAN'T OPEN THE DOOR!

WAY OUT

PULL

PERHAPS IF YOU OPENED IT THE PROPER WAY IT MIGHT HELP!

WAY OUT

PUSH!

LET ME BE AT THE FRONT OF THE TEAM—I'M BEST LOOKING!

HOI!

...CHAPPIES!

THIS IS ALL YOUR FAULT!

SNARL! PEST!

LET US THUMP HIM!

NO—LET ME HAVE HIM!

GROAN! LOOKS LIKE IT'S A "PLUG-OF-WAR" NOW!

FUN'S ALL THE FASHION

THINK I'LL PRESENT A FASHION AWARD AT THE SCHOOL.

TOOTS

FASHION MAG

At School—

WHY DO YOU WEAR THAT DREADFUL JERSEY?

IT MAKES A G JOLLY ROGER WE PLAY PIRA

SO I CAN BANDAGE MY KNEE WHEN I TRIP OVER IT!

WEARING YOUR CAP BACK TO FRONT ISN'T VERY FASHIONABLE. WHY DO YOU DO IT, PLUG?

TO SAVE WATER GOING DOWN MY NECK!

SPLOT!

...BECAUSE OUR WASHING GOT MIXED UP WITH THAT MAN'S IN THE LAUNDERETTE!

CHOKE!

WHY DO YOU WEAR GLASSES, 'ERBERT? CONTACT LENSES ARE MUCH MORE FASHIONABLE.

BECAUSE YOU CAN'T DAZZLE GOALIES WITH CONTACT LENSES!

WAH!

DAZZLE

GOAL!

THAT BLACK BLUE JERS LOOKS AWFUL, SI

ERK!

PEAS

PURELY FOR PROTECTION!

TEE-HEE! I SEE!

I CAN'T GET MY SHOES ON.

SILLY BOY.

EH?

FIZZLE!

MY ICE-CREAM! WHAT IS THE MEANING OF THIS?

MEL·T·

IT'S UNLUCKY IF YOU DON'T THROW SPILT SALT OVER YOUR SHOULDER!

SUPERSTITIOUS HOGWASH!

T! WHAT NOW?

WE'D HAVE SEVEN YEARS BAD LUCK IF PLUG'S FACE CRACKED THE MIRROR!

Then—

MORE SUPERSTITIOUS POPPYCOCK! HMM! IT'S RAINING.

PLOP!

GLUE

JUST A MINUTE—I'M INSIDE!

AN'T PUT UP AN BRELLA INSIDE—ERY UNLUCKY!

UST CART

Next morning—

WHERE ARE THOSE PUPILS?

DRUM! DRUM!

BASH ST.

SNORE!

DANNY'S HOUSE

ZZZ!

PLUG'S HOUSE

I MIGHT HAVE KNOWN IT—THEY'RE STILL IN BED!

YAHOO!

CKY BLACK CAT! T MUST CANCEL T FRIDAY THE HIRTEENTH!

So—

THIS IS OUR LUCKY DAY!

Later—

HERE'S THE FISH I PROMISED YOU, WINSTON! THAT SOOT COVERED YOUR WHITE PATCHES PERFECTLY!

TREASURE TRAIL

SIR W.C. BASH!

THIS IS HANGING SQUINT!

1. It was a special day indeed at Bash Street School. No, I didn't have more than Cuthbert's homework answers correct — it was 'Founder's Day'.

I took class IIb to view the portrait of 'Sir W. C. Bash', the man who founded Bash Street School as a place for the poor and unfortunate all those years ago.

Seeing the portrait brought a lump to my throat, as no-one's more poor and unfortunate than me having to teach those fiendish kids.

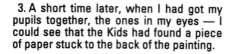

2. Danny decided to help straighten up the painting. Danny's 'help' only brought the painting down to land — yes, on poor old me!

So, not only had I a lump in my throat, I also had one on my head!

3. A short time later, when I had got my pupils together, the ones in my eyes — I could see that the Kids had found a piece of paper stuck to the back of the painting.

4. I would have to read this letter for the Kids. Joined up lettering will be taught some time in the future — say fifty years time!

However, I did discover it was from Sir W. C. Bash himself to be opened on a 'rainy day'.

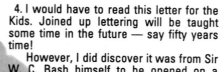

5. It was a 'Treasure Map', leading to a vast fortune, left by Sir W. C. Bash for the good of Bash Street School.
No lessons today — we were going on a 'Treasure Hunt'!

6. On reading the first instruction, we were stumped. The hunt was to begin at a tree planted by W. C. in the courtyard of the school. The very spot where the new gym had been build.

7. Ahem! The Kids were not to be stopped and began to try and find the stump of the old tree. Well, I suppose the gym floor is a bit unnecessary anyway — the little monkeys like to swing about on ropes above the floor at P.E. time.

8. After the dust settled, we did find the old tree stump. The hunt could begin, which is more than can be said for the next gym class!

9. As I was counting off the one hundred and fifty paces from the stump, some one else was counting too.

. . .78 . . .79 . . .80 . . .

. . .101 . . .102 . . .103 . . .

10. I then discovered it was Fatty keeping a tally of how many sausages he had in his mouth!

11. One hundred and fifty steps meant that we should have been at a stairway to the old clock tower. We had come to the end of the hunt — the stairway must have been bricked up years ago!

12. Luckily for us the brick wasn't as thick as Smiffy's head. The hunt was still on!

13. Plug was sent up the stairway first. Something had to scare away the nasty rats and things. Nothing better than Plug's mug!

THUD!

CLICK!

14. We reached the top of the tower at last. No one had been up here for some time and it looked as if it would be some time before we could leave. Fatty leaned back against the door and locked it.

PUSH

15. I had a bright idea. Ring the old bell to attract attention and be rescued. So I gave the bell a mighty heave.

DONG!

16. WAHEY! I'd hit the jackpot with one bell! Tied to the clapper was Sir W. C. Bash's fortune in gold!

CREAK! CREAK! CREAK! THUD!

CRASH!

17. Suddenly the value of gold was going down and us with it! A drop through the floor was the quick way down from the tower, but it was the sudden halt at the bottom which worried me!

WHEEE!

18. The Head came along to discover the gold and us. Already I could see he was thinking of ways of spending it.

A holiday in the sun, a fleet of staff cars, the hiring of a new cook . . .

19. . . . HUMPH! No such luck! The Head was spending the treasure on repairs to the school building. Damage he said had been caused during our 'Treasure Hunt'.

Huh! That's the Head off my Christmas card list for the next one hundred years!

20. And so it was back to searching for more hidden treasure for me, only this time there was as much chance of finding it as there is of Dennis the Menace winning the Nobel Peace Prize.

I was correcting the Kids' homework books and finding a correct answer made discovering the lost treasure seem as easy as blinking an eye.

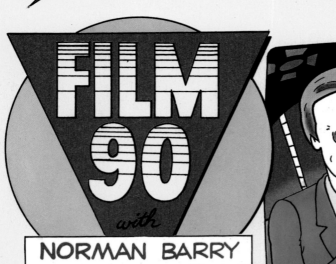

SOME FAMOUS FILMS HAVE BEEN REMADE BY BASH STREET CHARACTER — AND WHY NOT?

The GOOD   The BAD   The UGLY

SPLOSH!

CREAK!

JAWS

OH, DEAR! BOYS WILL BE BOYS!

TWANG! SPLAT!

ROTTEN EGGS

GOOD SHOT!

I DON'T THINK THIS LITTLE GIRL ENJOYED THE PRANK!

FLOUR

OLIVE

A YOUNG OLIVE THE TEA LADY!

A TIDY MINDED PUPIL WAS ALWAYS HANDY!

IT'S THE JANITOR AS A BOY!

TUT-TUT! WHAT A NAUGHTY LAD!

TREACLE

AND SO THAT ENDS A TYPICAL DAY IN BASH STREET SCHOOL 1946!

UGH!

I DIDN'T KNOW TILL THIS DAY IT WAS YOU WHO POURED TREACLE INTO MY MORTAR BOARD!

ER . . . MY OLD TEACHER!

DO 1,000,000 LINES, NAUGHTY BOY!

CHORTLE!

I must not pour treacle into mortar boards
I must not pour treacle into mortar

HMM!

Bash Street Teacher's note:—The gamekeeper told me about those pesky kids—they won't get away with it!

MAD HATTERS

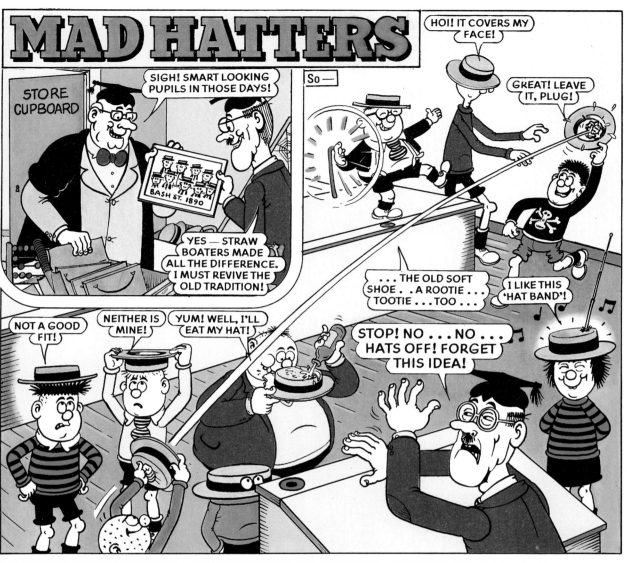

JUST LOOK AT THE SORT OF THINGS THE SCHOLARS OF TODAY CARRY THEIR BOOKS IN!

WHY DON'T YOU CHILDREN USE PROPER SCHOOLBAGS?

THESE ARE VERY HANDY...

THIS CANVAS BAG IS VERY USEFUL!

IN WHAT WAY?

SCHOOL KITCHEN WINDOW

SOUP

PRUNES AND CUSTARD

YUMMY!

BECAUSE FATTY EATS LIKE A HORSE...

...AND THIS MAKES A FINE NOSEBAG!

CHOMP! GUZZLE!

...er daft Smithy—

I CARRY MY BOOKS UNDER MY ARM!

BUT THAT'S A DOG!

GASP! OH, NO! THAT MEANS MUM'S TAKEN MY BOOKS FOR A WALK!

KNOW WHAT I USE MY BAG FOR?

NO!

CLASS II B

...uch later—

I'VE TRIED COUNTING SHEEP, BUT THEY FELL ASLEEP BEFORE I DID!

ZZZ!

Next morning—

LOOK AT TEACHER'S BAGS...

...UNDER HIS EYES, THAT IS!

THE SECRET'S OUT

Early one morning—

IT SAYS HERE THAT LOTS OF OLD BUILDINGS HAVE SECRET ROOMS AND PASSAGES IN THEM.

At Bash Street School—

O.
W. RALE
J. CAES
W. SHAK

THESE NAMES WOULD SUGGE SCHOOL IS FAIRLY OLD!

HOW CAN WE FIND OUT HOW TO FIND SECRET ROOMS?

SCRATCH

I KNOW!

WE'LL RING LORD SNOOTY AND ASK!

GREAT IDEA! BUNKERTON CASTLE MUST BE FULL OF SECRET ROOMS.

So—

YOU HAVE TO TAP THE WALLS AND LISTEN FOR HOLLOW SOUNDS.

THANKS A LOT, SNOOTY!

RU
RU
RU

AS I THOUGHT—NO BRAIN IN THERE!

HOLLOW SOUND!

GO AND PUT THESE TAPS AWAY!

WATCH THAT GLUE-POT, SMIFFY!

GLUE

TRIP

OOPS! HE DIDN'T!

JUST A MINUTE—WHERE DID YOU GET ALL THOSE STONES FROM?

OVER THERE!

GOODNESS! SURELY NOT ANOTHER SECRET ROOM?

IT'S A SECRET PASSAGE!

SOMEBODY'S COMING WITH A TORCH! WHO ON EARTH IS IT?

BIG SPENDERS

WISH OUR SCHOOL WAS GOOD AT SOMETHING—WE NEVER WIN ANY TROPHIES.

BUT WE ARE BEST AT SOMETHING, YOUR HEADSHIP!

WE ARE? WHAT?

COLLECTING WO SPOONS FOR CO LAST!

At the gala— BANG!

BOUNCE

And—

BOUNCE

BLOIK!

GASP! THE WINNER!

Presently—

YOU WILL COMPETE I THE SCHOOLS JUDO AN KARATE CONTEST.

JOLLY GOOD—I'M OF CHINESE FOO

GROAN! NO CHA

DIM PUPIL

The debate begins—

DANNY OF BASH STREET WILL PUT HIS POINTS FIRST.

SCHOOLS' DEBATING CONTEST

I'M RIGHT AND YOU'RE WRONG! ANYONE DISAGREE?

SCHOOLS' DEBATING CONTEST

N—NO! ANYTHING Y—YOU S—SAY!

SHUD

TREMBLE

QUAKE

SCHOOLS' DEBATING CONTEST

I CANNOT HIT A CHAP WITH GLASSES! I RETIRE!

HAR-HAR! I KNEW ALL THE OTHER BOYS WOULD BE TOO POLITE TO HIT 'ERBERT!

Later—

YOU'D BETTER WEAR THESE, TO SAVE YOU BEING DAZZLED!

OH, JOY! MY WISH COME TRU

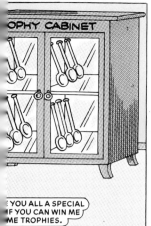

SEE THAT, KIDS? THEY'RE WEARING THE SAME TIE WHICH MEANS THEY BOTH WENT TO THE SAME SCHOOL. YES— VERY USEFUL THING, "THE OLD SCHOOL TIE"!

THIS WAY, YOUNG MAN. YOU'VE GOT THE JOB!

WAA!

CLANG!

MY TIE MAKES A GREAT "SLINGSHOT"! CHORTLE!

WHEEE!

PING!

HUMPH!

... IS TO HIDE MY EYES FROM THE KIDS!

WHEEE!

BOOT!

TOOT! PHEEP!